Process Improvement for Service Businesses

Unleashing Your Company's Brilliance

KATHLEEN HURLEY

Copyright © 2016 Kathleen Hurley

All rights reserved.

ISBN: 1537205951
ISBN-13: 978-1537205953

DEDICATION

This book is dedicated to my Dad, who taught me the joy of solving problems and puzzles, and who always expects me to deliver the best puns possible.

And to all those mentors who trusted me with their businesses and with their flow charts.

CONTENTS

1	The Business Divided	8
2	Organizational Systems	12
3	Begin Unleashing Brilliance	16
4	Begin Where You Are	22
5	Gather the Troops	32
6	The Flow	38
7	The Schedule	44
8	Communication	52
9	The Concept of Fail	64
10	Re Vision	72
11	Troubleshooting	79
12	Resources	83

1 THE BUSINESS DIVIDED

On their own, division and dissent are not negatives. They can promote growth, spur change and challenge settled thinking. When division and dissent appear in particular stages of a business cycle, they can interfere with the synergies that make a company run well. When a company has been built upon what works without the establishment of a defined process, growing pains can feel particularly acute. Some means by which disruption can occur:

The Family Company

Sometimes employees of firms going through a period of dissent say they feel as if there's a divorce underway. The family feel, the pull-together work ethic, and the sense that everyone at the firm shares a vision can be easily disrupted because those concepts are founded upon a shared trust. As the company grows, new people with new perspectives can create a landscape that feels like it's constantly shifting. Insecurity in an organization that once felt extremely stable and home-like can disrupt the trust that made the organization great.

The Growing Concern

It is not uncommon for a business to halve itself as it grows. Service becomes one side of the business, and sales becomes the other. If a brand takes off with a sufficient velocity and without a foundation in well-designed process, the division can cause lasting harm, with neither side respecting the vital work performed by the other.

The Slowing Platform

The market forces that drive our companies to grow can be cyclical in nature. No one single up-swing will last forever. Understanding the business cycle can mean predicting accurately the opportunities and challenges that are around the corner. Understanding the business cycle can also mean that new forces modify the cycle, sneak up on you, and send your company toward a decline in fortunes. Once perceived, this decline can be remedied. It takes some courage to understand when and what changes need to be made, but improving process definition can reduce waste, cut costs and better align resources inside an organization, in a recovery or before disaster hits.

The Economy, Stupid

In recent years, we've all had cause to look across a board room table and mutter or scream about the economy. The company that fully understands its processes can rebound quickly when market forces change, adjusting and responding to changes in monetary, regulatory and economic forces. By no means can all challenges be overcome by process definition. But starting with a firm understanding of where you are gives you an opportunity to define where you are going.

Failure

A lost client. A lost *major* client. Bad press. Reputational damage. Social media drama. Employee exodus.

Failure is not pretty. A business culture which has grown up around success, particularly a service business, is going to respond poorly to failure. When the hits keep on coming, it can be challenging to find enough energy and faith inside the organization to move forward, unless there is a clear definition of the company's reason for being. What does the firm do, exactly, and why?

Knowing the mission and vision and working processes of a company can provide an antidote to failure, and a prescription for iterative improvement.

When a business finds itself encountering any of these issues, it has no response. The business under pressure is literally and figuratively silent.

That is because a business, in and of itself, and as much as it feels as though it should be different, cannot make decisions. The leaders in the business are responsible for making decisions. And make no mistake, leaders are everywhere within an organization, not just at the board or managerial level.

> *A leader is best when people barely know he exists, when his work is done, his aim fulfilled, they will say: we did it ourselves.*
>
> *-Lao Tzu*

Particularly as businesses grows, or when a business are led by a particularly dynamic entrepreneurial force, there can be a vacuum of information at the top. It's easy to know what a company sells. It's more complicated to understand how, exactly, the clients are served. The magic behind the scenes just happens, for some leaders, and trusted subordinates ensure that it keeps on happening.

While this method works just fine, it means that upper level decisions are being taken based on a lack of information. Polices are made without full understanding of what it takes to serve the client. Worse, sales are made without a full understanding of what can be delivered to the client. Senior leaders may react to situations they don't fully understand, creating regulations that go against the best interests of the firm.

When a leader is ensconced in an organization that has not been designed to absorb and appreciate the input of the entire team, without a framework for accepting change and lacking a way to safely challenge the status quo, there is going to be very little that will get the necessary facts to the most senior people who need them.

The example of the isolated leader illustrates the true nature of a company divided: it isn't the divisional rivalries, or a lack of trust in the ranks, or a failure to document that will bring down a firm in the midst of a crisis or cause leadership to allow an inflection point to sweep by unrecognized. It isn't even a lack of team work that can create problems for the bottom line. It is a lack of organizational communication which can create client dissatisfaction, organizational stagnation and sales declines. The company that thinks together stays together.

KATHLEEN HURLEY

2 ORGANIZATIONAL SYSTEMS

They change with the times. The traditional management models still exist, with complicated management models, matrix relationships that hardly make sense and strict vertical hierarchies, they are inflexible and inefficient.

The scientific management models overcome many of the traditional flaws, allowing for more self-directed work with less hierarchical reporting and an emphasis on a three hundred and sixty degree view of the workplace. While the scientific management models seem to revise and re-release every few years, they have much in common. Those managers who have been around long enough will have seen TQM, Six Sigma, Lean, Agile, Devops, and countless other frameworks that purport to manage a company in the most efficient, scientific way possible.

Scientific management models have flaws. They are difficult for some people to understand. They require a more engaged, more logic-literate and self-directed workforce. For workers and managers who thrive on big wins and visible success, there is a flatness to the scientific model that can be demotivating. Employees can perceive the scientific model as cold and focused only on the bottom line.

For an organization that is predicting change, however, the scientific management model is a means to standardization and alignment of resources. It is a demanding approach that does necessitate employee engagement, but that engagement produces a more highly educated and more logically trained workforce. In addition to offering a stable and knowable business backbone, the scientific management model offers employees an unprecedented opportunity to contribute to the organization and level up their careers.

This book focuses on a form of scientific management theory. It is not based on any one particular management model, but harnesses thinking and design from several. In fact, it harnesses the most shared characteristics of the most adopted scientific management models of the last sixty-five years.

In the past the man has been first; in the future the system must be first... The first object of any good system must be that of developing first class men.

-Frederick W. Taylor

Because most scientific management systems grew out of a need to make manufacturing more operationally efficient, responsive and flexible, there have been critics of these management models who have said they are hardly relevant any longer. As the economy has transitioned away from manufacturing and has become more centered on service, some people think that scientific management models simply cannot be applied organically to service organizations.

Without undertaking to directly refute that assertion, this book will present a business leader with a simple path by which to embed the best of the scientific management models into a service organization. It is meant to offer a flexible and malleable system which can be easily understood, quickly applied, and measurably evaluated by any service company.

A service organization, for the purposes of this book, is defined as a company which does not manufacture. A service organization can, and often does, include sales professionals. Such an organization could even be a part or segment of a manufacturing company. But for the purposes of this discussion, the creation of a product or good is kept separate and apart.

Established service companies face some severe challenges in today's markets. These challenges extend across most developed nations, cultures and social structures.

The framework by which customers are obtained and retained has completely shifted with the internet revolution. There is less brand loyalty than marketing economists have recorded in prior times. The customers with the most to spend are the most savvy, tuned in to value and ready to walk customers, and service organizations are not accustomed to handling their new approach. In short, there is pressure on the demand side.

There are constraints on the supply side, as well. For example, professional services companies are now competing outside their vertical for talent. Where recruiters for the best business students could once count on culling their applicants from particular business programs at particular schools, those same recruiters are now faced with Technology majors who want to run firms, and Business students who want to teach Literature. There is more overlap, less respect for swim lanes, and a more pervasive sense of entrepreneurial spirit in the Gen-X, Gen Y and Millennial generations. Sometimes this translates as self-absorption, a lack of respect and a level of arrogance. Sometimes that's accurate. Finding the right people to serve as leaders, or to groom as leaders, in a service company is more difficult than it has been in recent memory.

And all of this is change bolstered by fundamentals that are shifting on a seemingly hourly basis. Companies in the transport services industries have had to deal with the emergence of threats that were never legally possible before as Uber and its descendants have encroached upon long held territory. Companies that have been built to serve regulated industry scramble as the regulations change every three weeks, and new knowledge of what's expected is gained the hard way. Those firms that have been able to meet customer needs by harnessing new technologies were once the top of the heap. Now they scramble to prevent data loss, hacking and customer distrust.

Service companies have never had it easy. They have also never seen the level of opportunity being presented by this marketplace disruption. The change in consumer expectations, both in the retail and business to business service sectors, cannot be allowed to fly past unharnessed. The company that is able to define who it is, what it does, and do it best, is the one that will rise above the current chaotic environment.

The aim of this book is simple: to provide a tool for an organization to understand its mission and values, know what it has as resources in its pocket, and define what it does every day. Then this book will offer some modest recommendations for what to do with that knowledge once the company has gained it.

A business with a management model does not have all the cards and is not guaranteed a win. A business with a management model has opportunity. An extra chance to rise above, to see things more clearly than the competition and to do better for those it serves. Isn't that what it's all about, anyway?

3 BEGIN UNLEASHING BRILLIANCE

The following chapters will outline the necessary steps to take to start the process of defining process. The instructions are intended to be simple and straightforward. There are worksheets that are included at the end of the book that are referenced in the text, but included separately so they can be photocopied and used repeatedly. It is intended to be used more than once, passed around, and made into practical use.

Using the book in a step by step manner is a good way to use it the first time. Once the process improvement cycle has been completed one time, it may not be necessary to go through every chapter every time.

Preparing for The Process

Getting yourself, as a leader, into the right mindset to approach process improvement is the first step toward gathering your assets. As with most things, beginning the cycle with a look at one's self is a good way to start.

A leader, no matter where he falls on the org chart, is going to be put in a position of trust during the process improvement cycle. He will be making decisions that will impact the lives and livelihoods of his coworkers and friends, and the marketplace at large. Often the pressure of this process is interpreted by those who are not included to mean that jobs are on the line. Being able to communicate the meaning of the process improvement cycle, which is solely to improve the workflows in the organization, is very important.

> *Excellent firms don't believe in excellence - only in constant improvement and constant change.*
>
> *-Tom Peters*

Leaders have different points of failure in their own internal systems of thought and response. For some leaders, the idea that their business requires improvement is difficult. For many leaders, there can be a sense of personal investment in the business that causes criticism of the business to transfer automatically to criticism of the leader. That is a natural effect for some leaders. Understanding up front if this is a trap into which you can personally fall is one way to prepare for the inevitable. The process improvement cycle should be kept positive at all times, but a leader who is this invested in the company could feel a twinge at some of the suggestions for change that might arise.

Other leaders are susceptible to a sense that they understand what's going on at all levels of the organization. In some cases, they are correct. Especially in the earlier stages of a company, the leadership will have a very firm understanding of what is done, because often they are doing all of the work! This should not stop such a leader from proceeding through the process. There are different, creative realizations that can come from working through a system. A leader with a deep understanding of the processes their company utilizes will have more of these epiphanies. Those leaders who are more removed from the back end of the workflow should ensure that they are not riding on old assumptions about how things used to be done.

For those leaders who are starved for time, stretched in many different directions, and nearing the territory of unhealthy work-life balance, this process improvement cycle is probably one of the most important undertakings possible. There are certainly meetings that are long, and added work that needs to be done as a result of the process improvement cycle. However, the investment of time is a small price to pay to recapture the opportunities of the business. In fact, some companies that have gone through this process have found time as a result, allowing critical staff to return to more normal sleep cycles!

Leaders who think that their business suffers from staff that is not the right staff may find the process unconformable. Failure to hire properly is almost never the only issue in a business suffering from disruption. Likewise, those who are certain that they already know the changes that should be made to improve the business will need to loosen their minds a bit to approach the process with a positive, open and listening bent.

Trusting the Process

There are some structural frameworks that should be followed when engaging in process improvement. Understanding that the process improvement process is not one that ends, it should be clear the importance of beginning as you mean to go on. The process improvement team that is assembled will change as people move through the organization, but the structure and social covenants of the team should not change.

First, set out to create an environment that is safe for all of the participants to be honest. This should involve removing any hierarchical tendencies that the organization has overall. In other words, when the process improvement team steps into the room, they leave their titles behind and retain only their functional roles. There are no Vice Presidents of Sales or Senior Accountants. There are only representatives of the sales cycle and representatives of the accounting cycle.

Allow the room to be led by someone other than the most senior person in the room. Some companies choose to alternate the meeting leadership, and this can work well. In companies that are suffering from a great deal of distrust, however, it can be more helpful to have consistency in the team's leadership.

Encourage a culture of listening and asking questions politely and appropriately. Defining a process must involve the people who do the work. They are the only ones who know intimately which links are clicked, when calls are made and how bills are paid. Take the approach that it is a privilege to spend time with these people who make your company move forward every day. Any sense that you, as a leader, are distracted, resentful or stressed by the process will communicate itself to your other team members.

Once the participants in the room have begun to feel that something is off-center with a leader, they will respond in ways that may be obvious to you if you are looking for the signs. You may feel the meetings lose their energy. You may find that the staff is responding as a unit, rather than thinking and generating new ideas as individuals. You may find yourself suddenly surrounded by Yes Men and Yes Women. These may be symptoms that something has been perceived as threatening. Your team has engaged a fear response. Look to yourself and the other leaders in the organization to ensure that your unconscious behavior has not created this response and take immediate and active steps to reassure the team that they are valued and their input is critical.

It has long been said that there are no stupid questions. This is patently and demonstrably untrue, as documented in numerous internet memes. However, one way to encourage trust is to agree with the team that there will be no incorrect answers during brainstorming. Another method is to banish the concept of failure from the room. Yet another path toward quickly building the creative energy of the group involves removing personal names from the process and only discussing roles and functions.

No matter what appeals to you as a method to keep the team together and moving, your role as a business leader on a process improvement team is to first keep yourself in control of yourself, and second to ensure that the team is functioning at maximum capacity.

Roles and Rules

Process improvement team structures will vary by organization. A service company that has fifteen different, highly defined lines of service will likely start out with smaller divisional teams that come together as a larger team later on. A service company that is mid-sized, with up to 500 employees, will probably start as one unit. The structure should represent the organization. Those who work in a functional role can be brought in as experts to help the core team when needed, or they can be made a fixture on the team if their input is regularly required. There is no limit to the size of the team, although teams of no more than about ten members seem to reach the highest level of functionality.

The team will require a few people to serve in team leadership capacities. A scribe, or note taker, is absolutely required. Even if using methods like video recording during the meeting, there will be stages during the process when it's simply easier to see what is being discussed when it's written down. Elect the scribe first.

When determining a person to facilitate the meeting, as previously suggested, try to avoid using those who already serve in leadership positions at an organizational level. Rather, allow the facilitator to be someone who can listen openly for dissent, redirect conversations well, and help move the meeting along if it stalls. Some organizations find success in rotating the meeting facilitator. In this pattern, the facilitator should not be a person who has a strongly vested motivation in the day's topic of conversation. Because they are removed from the impacts of the workflowing discussion, they can ask questions and stir discussion without preconceived notions getting in their way.

Equipment and Supplies

There is no wrong way to conduct a process improvement meeting, provided that all team members feel represented and heard and have trust in the process. However, there are some tools which are helpful to the cause. The next section attempts to suggest a range of ways in which to approach a particular exercise with different tools, for companies with different resource levels.

Show Your Work

One of the difficulties of having a process is communicating that process to others who don't perform it. As people who are in the weeds discuss the particulars of getting one client's needs met, they use shorthand because they understand the process completely in their minds. One of the dangers of that shorthand is that steps are skipped verbally, which can communicate an inaccurate process to someone less familiar with the flow. When reviewing process, it is important to show exactly what is being discussed so that logical inconsistencies can be filled in and understood by all parties. A piece of paper taped to the wall or a laptop projected on a screen can each be great formats for recording the proceedings. The laptop has the addition of flexibility. Even using Word Processing software to create flow charts, boxes can be moved around and inserted easily in real-time. Paper can become messy but if you find that things are out of control, a quick snapshot of the notes to date will help for reference when the flowcharts are transcribed.

Best Get Comfortable

Appreciating that there is no one way to accomplish this goal, it is best to make the team comfortable. For some companies that involves meeting offsite where team members won't be interrupted and can arrive in comfy clothes. For some companies, the sense of being removed from the office generates anxiety, and members benefit from the proximity to their normal workflows. For paper based businesses, having quick access to documents can be helpful in generating examples and conversation.

No matter how you accommodate the "Get Comfy" clause, make sure you are reinforcing your company's culture and general expectations with your choice. No matter your choice, remember that you are taking your employees out of their normal workflow and asking them to participate in a meeting that is going to be different from what most of them have done before. It will challenge the way they each work. It may feel nosey and weird. Keeping everyone at ease is one of the jobs of the leader. This does not require team building exercises, or forced ice breakers. It does require that everyone is introduced to everyone else, and that there is a clear understanding of what each person's functional role is and what team they represent. Beyond that, keep an eye out for behaviors that indicate discomfort, distrust or disengagement. They will keep you from reaching your goals, and you can proactively make connections to mollify those participants who are having difficulty adjusting to the team or to the process.

4 BEGIN WHERE YOU ARE

One of the reasons that these particular elements of scientific process have been selected is their implementation strategy. For most service organizations, it would mean a significant loss of custom (not to mention customer loyalty) if the company were to shut down business for three weeks in order to redesign and implement process.

For a new company that's just starting up, it is an great idea to implement a process management strategy from the outset. For those who have existing obligations to customers and employees, it is a little difficult to stop working in order to change the way you work. Therefore, this book's assumption is that your organization has work to do and will be in the weeds of doing that work while the process improvement cycle goes on.

Before the official meetings begin to happen, it is useful for the leaders in the organization to undertake some self-reflection. We've discussed some of the personal quirks that can get in the way of successful leadership participation in the process improvement cycle. Personalities are tough to change, even when the desire to do so is fully there. Being aware of the quirks that leaders (including yourself) bring to the meeting can help instill patience and even remind you of resources that some of your compatriots possess.

It is also helpful for the leadership to collectively consider the business itself. At the company's inception, there was probably the exercise of defining the mission, vision and values for the organization. Those foundational elements could have changed a bit since the company began, even though most consultants will tell you those principles are supposed to remain static. It could be that the mission, vision and values of the company are precisely what they were when the founding occurred. Either way, it's best to know at the outset of the cycle what you want to achieve. Understanding the customers you serve and how you want to be perceived internally as well as externally can be a very solid exercise.

Significant consultant time and dollars are spent when a company wants to define itself. The process may require a professional facilitator to act as an objective third party if there is a great deal of disruption happening in the organization. But it may be that a few leaders in the company are able to sit down and do a bit of work to outline what the company stands for. Here are some ways to approach a series of three one-hour meetings in which the company can define its reason for existing.

Preparing for Meeting One: The Mission Statement

Start-up companies sometimes struggle (or sometimes revel in!) the period in which they're finding themselves, trying out different strategies and concepts of how to market, what to sell and who to be. This is a fine way to approach business, and particularly in the tech sector, one that works flexibly and well.

For a company that is already in existence, it is probably easier to define its mission than it is for a concept company. The reason is that, as a leader in a going concern, you already know what it is that you do to bring in revenue. If the purpose of the company is to provide accounting services to other businesses, that is the thesis of the mission statement.

The suggestion of many professionals is that you begin the brainstorming process as though you don't know what the thesis statement is. Starting with a blank slate, it is suggested, can bring all sorts of ideas about what the company *could* be to the forefront. In this way, you might harness some of that tech start up passion, energy and creativity for a company that might be a little set in its ways. This can create all manner of digressions, and while they can be full of ideas that might prove useful later on down the road, if you're in a time crunch you could consolidate this step.

Busy leaders in operating companies will be more disposed to spend their time constructing the vision. Take advantage of that fact and use the first meeting to establish report, define the objectives of the process improvement process, and establish talking points that can help diffuse nerves throughout the organization.

Outstanding people have one thing in common: An absolute sense of mission.

-Zig Ziglar

Meeting One: The Mission Statement

Total Time: One Hour

Agenda: Define the goals of the process improvement cycle; describe the process improvement cycle as you will to employees; establish basic operating principles for the team; define the mission statement.

Defining the mission statement for a company can be a difficult exercise. Is it enough to say what you do? Probably not, but it's a great starting place. Using your visual brainstorming tools like a projected laptop or a piece of paper on the wall, write up the suggestions from the team. Here are some suggestions that might apply to that accounting services company:

Provide accounting services
Provide accounting solutions
Provide secure data management
Enable clients to trust their accounting team

The list can go on a bit once people get rolling. Keep this brainstorming part of the meeting to about 15 minutes.

Now encourage the team to construct one unified statement from the brainstorming items on the board. Make them aware at the outset that they have 15 minutes to conclude this process. They will likely arrive at a functional statement like:

Accounting Services Corp provides trustworthy and secure accounting services.

If the team hasn't arrived at a statement like this in 15 minutes, it is better to break and resume the meeting at a later time, when people have been able to think through the options. Make sure they brainstorming notes are distributed so they can be reviewed.

If the team is able to get to their draft statement, take the next 10 minutes to make sure it includes all of the adjectives and descriptors that the team wants. By a show of hands, make sure that everyone is satisfied with the statement. A majority is not enough – you are going for consensus.

Conclude the meeting and schedule the next one.

Preparing for Meeting Two: The Vision Statement

Describing a dream is tricky. If someone can't see the visuals in your mind, it's hard for most people to create a word picture. The same is true of defining a vision for a company. There is a lot of back and forth, and sometimes a fair bit of disagreement. For this reason, the Vision Statement meeting will be longer than Meeting One, as you are still reaching for consensus.

You will also probably feel a different cadence to this meeting. There is generally some introspection, and a sense that this isn't easy thinking that's being done. There will be more gaps in the conversation as participants mull over what has been said and prepare what they want to say. This is natural, and not a cause for concern.

However, if the meeting becomes in any way contentious, even passive aggressively so, facilitating the meeting can become interesting. In an environment where you are reaching for consensus, it is not possible to shut down dissent. Verbalized or otherwise expressed, dissent is critical to the evolution of consensus. However, there is a need to shut down disrespect in any form. Bringing the team to a point where they can express themselves in a non-hostile, active and positive framework is necessary practice for the meetings to come.

One way in which you can create the right mindset for this particular meeting is to use context. The individuals participating in the team may know each other quite well already or they may be relative strangers. In either case, asking them to participate in an exercise that will be revealing of self before they attend the meeting can open doors to a deeper connection with this aspect of the process, and with other team members. This does not mean that indulging in ice breaker games is a way to get everyone singing a camp fire song. Rather, opening the individual mind and offering the team the opportunity to address one another truthfully and in a somewhat more exposed manner can be useful in many ways.

Consider sending each team member the Myers-Briggs evaluation to be completed before the meeting. Then letter their four character code on their name tags, but do not address the experiment in any other way during the meeting. At the end of the meeting, reserve 20 minutes to review how the meeting ran, and see what sort of insights are revealed due to the exercise. They may be purely introspective results, and that is perfectly OK, but some teams have seen greater respect emerge for different perspectives and different communication styles when their basis was presented in a simple way.

Even if you elect a different way of breaking down barriers and getting people personally involved in creating the company's vision, asking participants to prepare before the meeting can help alleviate issues around communication. In this case, the vision that each person brings to the table will likely be somewhat unique, and will be predetermined. The meeting can be best spent reviewing, aligning and discussing.

Meeting Two: The Vision Statement

Total Time: Four Hours

Agenda: Reviewing prepared vision elements; coming to consensus on a vision statement.

By establishing a safe environment during the Mission Statement round, it is possible that the Vision Statement round will be entirely smooth and without issue. It is equally possible that, with the egos, baggage, worries and psychological dysfunction we all carry about each day, the Vision Statement round will be protracted and full of group dynamics to manage. Either way, the goal is the same. Producing a vision statement that unifies the team is a process that both harnesses and creates energy, and energy is what every company needs to push forward.

Begin by reviewing the vision elements each person has brought to the meeting. Record either their full statements or the key words and points on the visual board. Even though this exercise was completed individually, it serves as brainstorming. For that reason, there should be no discussion or debate of the elements at this point.

Once all of the vision elements have been read out and recorded on the board, take a break. This should be long enough for people to meet their immediate needs (visit the restroom, get a drink or snack) and also spend some time looking over the visual board. It should not be so long that people can wander away and get involved in other thought processes. Likewise, this is a point where alliances can form, if they are not already in existence. Making sure that there is a bit of time pressure will prevent people from caucusing during the break.

When the meeting reconvenes, make sure the recorded vision elements are visible, but also have a blank slate on which to begin the process of reconciling and consolidating the company's vision statement. It may be appropriate to remind the team that, while they came in with individual ideas of where the company should go, they are now tasked with creating one vision which everyone agrees upon. There should be no other agenda or stake in the game except to create the vision that most perfectly supports the mission statement everyone has already signed off on.

A Word About Consensus Building

As with so many things, people come to the vision meeting with intense feelings that they may not themselves fully understand. We've already talked about how so many leaders identify closely with the company they serve, and how that close identification can become a vulnerability. The vision meeting, because it asks participants to expose their dreams for the organization in an honest and creative way, can highlight those vulnerabilities.

It's been said that consensus building is an art. It is true that some people come to life with a great sense of grace and diplomacy. Those who are not so well endowed can take refuge in the fact that, while sarcasm and irony are almost never teachable, grace and diplomacy can be learned if there is a basis in empathy that already exists.

Be aware that building consensus means compromise. Compromise means potentially giving up something quite meaningful to the personal identity of one of your leaders. Be confident and careful, but also be thoughtful and caring. Your graceful presence can mean the difference between a successful vision for the company's future and a less driven, less energetic, less satisfying trajectory.

Concluding the vision statement is similar to wrapping up the mission statement. Ensure that you have achieved consensus. Determine if there are any flaws that need to be addressed. Give everyone time to read the vision statement silently, and also read it aloud, even multiple times. Once you are certain that the vision statement articulates the path that the company has chosen for its next cycle, you should circulate the vision statement for further review and study and close the meeting by scheduling the next one.

Preparing for Meeting Three: The Values

The mission statement sets out the destination of the company. The vision statement sets out the path that will be taken to get there. The values of the organization, then, set out the means of travel.

There is a reason that we react so strongly and unconsciously to companies and organizations. Our basis in understanding how groups of people work is formed in our own family structures. There is a hierarchy, there are expectations, there is punishment and reward. The organizations and companies that we create are going to have many of the same features that we know from our own childhoods. Because the knowledge of those systems is so deeply ingrained, there is sometimes an unconscious retrieval process that brings the roles and even the verbiage of our families up to the top of our adult working lives. Particularly when your service organization is led by deeply embedded professionals, or by owners as in a law firm, there can be a heightened, almost parental approach to this segment of thinking.

Values ultimately describe the manner in which people operate. Selecting defining values for your company means participants are asked to verbalize those values they hold dear, and in doing so, to expose some vulnerability to the group. When people are vulnerable, they are most likely to retreat to ingrained behavior. The same behavior patterns that came naturally in the family structure may not work as well in the board room. After all, swiftly kicking your sibling under the dinner table is not as uncommon as swiftly kicking your company President.

Nonetheless, people are people. Your leaders must be treated with respect and if there are issues that arise due to personal perspectives, it can be best to break the meeting, rather than try to push through. Do not take that to mean that personal thoughts, even when expressed emotionally, should be swept under the rug. To the extent possible, allow the group to explore the values that your professionals advocate.

Coming into the values meeting as a blank slate, rather than with prepared concepts, is generally the better way to approach the project. The company's values are not going to accurately and completely reflect the values of any one person on the team, unless it a one person team. Rather than set your leaders up for disappointment, it is better to create a space in which the values will be discussed at length and in a group setting.

Meeting Three: The Values

Total Time: Two Hours

Agenda: Brainstorming values; discussing values elements; creating a list of the company's core values.

Establishing the most important values of the organization is critical because it gives every employee a prescribed method in which to operate. It also shows the company's dedication to a way of behaving, and illuminates the covenants by which the employees and leaders of the firm will interact with one another.

Introducing the Values meeting with a brief description of what values mean can be helpful. Try to do so without using examples if you can. If you do need to use examples, try to bring them from other organizations' published values (do not use those of the competition!). In that way the participants can review what's been done before and feel confident about what they can create in this session.

Begin with a standard brainstorming session. Create your visual list of values that are suggested. Try to ensure that everyone in the room participates in the conversation. Create a visual board to reflect the brainstorming items as they come up. Avoid any discussion or conversation about the items, and assure participants that this will come later in the meeting.

Take a break after the brainstorming concludes, and come back to the meeting with a fresh page on which to work. Make sure that the values which have already been suggested are visible in the room. Limit the break appropriately.

The next step is different from what was done during the previous two stages. Rather than asking the group to come with a consensus-driven means to consolidate the values, you are going to first ask them which words on the board mean the same things. In other words, can your team agree that the value "integrity" encompasses the value "honesty" and that both do not need to be on the board? It is possible that the team cannot agree on this! There are nuances that are very important in word choice. But where the values which have been suggested are similar, try to combine them.

With the goal of getting down to no more than five values during this session, ask the team to discuss the ones that remain. It is possible that some of the remaining values are more personal values, and do not pertain to the organization. It is possible that some more values can be eliminated after discussion.

When it is clear that the elimination round has concluded and the values on the board are what is left, evaluate how many there are. There is no firm rule that you can only have five values. If your team's hard work has brought you down to six, you may decide that is perfectly acceptable! However, if you have twenty values remaining, you need to continue narrowing the field.

You can approach the remaining values with discussion (which can take some time, as the person with the value on the board may feel the need to present a very full and accurate word picture of what the value means), or you can approach the group by asking them to imagine what a company with a specific set of values (the ones on the board) would be like. What would it be like to sell that company's services? How would people who work in each department feel under those values? What would a customer's experience look like when they wanted to renew a contract? Is it possible that some values do not even pertain to the company at all?

By eliminating more of the board, you should be getting closer to your goal. Open up the floor to anyone who wants to discuss removing one of the value words from the board. Allow the change cycle to continue until complete, although stay within the overall allotted meeting time. If you cannot reach consensus on the values within the meeting time, schedule a follow up meeting. Schedule the next meeting in the not-distant future, as the process benefits from concentrated thought without interruption from the outside world.

When you have completed your list of values, write them down and circulate them with the Mission and Vision statements. Ask the team to review them and be prepared to authorize them as the final version, or recommend changes within a week.

Always stick with your schedule. Circulate an email or other appropriate means for your team to authorize the mission, vision and values within a week.

5 GATHER THE TROOPS

It may seem backward, but there was a purpose in describing the business definition cycle before the of the process improvement cycle.

Understanding the roles that need to be played, how the various meetings in the business development stage can play out and some of the psychology that creates the environment of the meetings can positively prepare you for selecting the team you need to handle the work of process improvement.

Of course, the team selection process should not be left up to just one person. There is a strict need to include representation from each department, even if there is no individual that strikes you as particularly suited to this work. The leadership circle that assembles to create the mission and vision statements should all have a hand in approving the team that appears for the first round of process improvement.

Some companies keep a succession team or leadership growth team assembled at all times. If it is the case that this group exists and is representative of the need for all departments to have a say, then this could be the easy route to selecting your team.

However, in some companies the process of assembling the team becomes political and contentious. Professionals who facilitate such events strongly suggest that the process not resemble a competitive reality television show. If there are nominations to be made and a vote to be taken, ensure that the ballots are anonymous, and that there is no stumping for any one candidate. In fact, there are some who suggest rotating candidates through the meetings. While this can result in some rework and tenuous team alignment, it may be the strategy of last resort for a group that is highly divided.

Ensuring that the key participants, or the "core team" are comprised of those who run your back office systems will serve you well. Make sure that Accounting, Human Resources, Information Technology and Legal are represented. They are all systems-driven professionals with different perspectives, knowledge and experience. More importantly, they are accustomed to being creative, working with the resources at hand, and ensuring successful outcomes.

As you navigate through the rest of your life, be open to collaboration. Other people and other people's ideas are often better than your own. Find a group of people who challenge and inspire you, spend a lot of time with them, and it will change your life.

-Amy Poehler

Identifying Departmental Representation

It's easy to say that departmental representation is required, but it can be far more difficult to fairly arrange such a thing. The service company that has not grown to a level where specialists are confined to strict swim lanes will have the hardest time. During the most intense growth phases of a company's existence, the best employees wear the most hats. There is no denying that some of most highly flexible, very promising organizations have five percent of their workforce doing twenty percent of the work (or more!). When selecting people to represent different work groups, it can seem like a short cut to grab a few of those five percenters and call it a day. After all, they know exactly what's going on anyway, and they can speak for others easily.

There are two inherent down sides to this strategy. First, the factual. When those five percenters say they know how things are being run, they are probably right on some specific levels. It is not often, however, that they are completely able to know what is actually happening. That is to say, they know how things are supposed to go, and possibly how they do go eighty percent of the time. The other twenty percent will be a black box to them. This group is the most likely to be taken by surprise during the process improvement cycle. They tend to be systems thinkers who can move very quickly and multitask well. While creative, they do not unnecessarily deviate from their defined process. To do so would be less efficient, they would argue. In this process improvement cycle, this personality type brings a weakness to the table in that they are sure. Overloading the process improvement cycle with systems logicians will only create an inauthentic and useless series of flow charts that do not reflect reality.

The second reason is less factual and more political. Your company is made up of people who come to work every single day to do their best. Starting with that assumption, you can recognize that there are people who will take it as an honor and a privilege to participate in the process improvement team. There are also people who will be frightened out of their wits the moment they are asked to take part. But if you ask no one from a department, the response will be quick and definitive across the group: they will feel rejected and left out. This is not the kind of response you want to engender in your workforce at any time, much less a critical juncture like process improvement time. Invite a representative from each team and ensure that you have the respect, accountability and buy-in from each team. Without it, your process improvement cycle is not likely to implement well.

Departmental Versus Functional Representation

In many mature organizations, there are departments that contain multiple functional roles. There can be receptionists in the same department with customer service professionals. These people perform vastly different work functions within the organization, appear at different places in the value stream, and define different processes because of it. "Department" cannot always be taken as short hand for "Function" but it is used almost everywhere in process improvement.

The reason is sizing. In some companies, having functional representation rather than departmental representation would mean every single person on the organization participating in process improvement.

Think about that in the context of your company. Could every single person participate, at some level, in the process improvement cycle?

The answer is yes. It has to be. No matter what size the company is, or how you structure your representation at the core of each meeting, there is no excuse for allowing the cycle to go on without the input from and buy-in of the staff. This will be achieved by the end, but for now, consider sizing as your only significant constraint.

Teams that are too large will be ineffective. Teams that are too small will be ignorant. The sizing for a process improvement core team seems best between 10 and 15 members. If this accommodates one single representative from each department, then you are in luck! Begin the selection process.

If your service organization can't begin to make 15 people comprise departmental representation, divide and conquer is the rule of the day. If your company has regional or other geographic divisions, have each division establish their own core team and elect a representative to the organization-wide group. If you have different office locations where the same departments are housed, do the same. Create a way by which each department is represented on some level, and then bring the resulting work together at a higher, organizational level.

The Secret Society

In an effort to keep the peace in the organization, and because some leaders perceive necessary change as failure, it's an instinctual response to keep the membership lists of the teams secret. This is understandable, but undermines the process completely. If the organization cannot stand the idea of change to such an extent that they are unable to embrace improvement, it is best to stop here and make plans to call in a professional.

Allowing the company as a whole transparency into the process improvement cycle not only ensures that there will be less fear and resentment about what can be seen as job-threatening, but also that there will be active participation and conversation about how things can be better. Creating an environment in which every single member of the team is free to contribute to making the company as efficient and effective as possible is critical to corporate success.

That being said, it is not necessary to publish a newsletter or post results after every meeting. The process improvement cycle being an ongoing part of the company's well-being means that it should integrate into the consciousness and culture of employees in an organic fashion. Communicate about the progress as you would any other major initiative, but do not go out of your way to draw attention to it.

Avoiding the Clear Winners

There are employees in every organization who stand out above the rest. They are perhaps the ones who do the most, or do it best, or do it with the most style. They are above average.

In the process improvement cycle, you need these winners to be active participants. Not only will they contribute valuable information to the team, but they will also be natural leaders in their groups and will be able to disseminate information with authority and clarity.

However, they should not be the only members of the team representing their departments. The poor performers, the vastly mediocre and those who hardly seem to care should also be invited to the team, if only as functional experts on the day their work area is reviewed. Their input is just as critical as the input of those who stand above the rest and feeling included has rarely created a bad work product.

Structuring and Scheduling Meetings

Working around work is one of the more difficult aspects of hosting an engaged and productive process improvement team. The process requires as much flexibility and consideration as possible for those who are serving in two jobs at once.

On the encouraging side, the product that comes from the meetings will surely reduce the workload on the team overall, and most of the team members will realize this very quickly. Reinforcing this foundational concept can help keep the energy up in the room, and keep people from feeling overwhelmed during the process.

There will likely be those who attempt to bring their work to the meeting. After all, there are going to be times during which their pet workflow moments are not being discussed, and they'd like to toss off a few emails during those moments. Unfortunately, the entire group dynamic can be disrupted by that kind of disengagement. Encourage a meeting venue with no technology allowed, leaving phones, laptops and tablets at the door. If setting an example doesn't cause this to take, state the requirement aloud. It's important enough that everyone stay engaged to cause a little tech-withdrawal. It will ultimately play out to the benefit of the company overall.

One method that companies have used to some success is to start the first process improvement meeting by creating a set of team bylaws. These can state anything from the desired outcomes to the way in which people will behave. Respecting deadlines, communicating clearly and without judgement, removing names and using roles instead and other rules of the road can quickly become ingrained if they are issued by the group as a whole.

6 THE FLOW

Finally – it seems like it's taken forever, right? – you arrive at the moment when your team is assembled. Your visual board is ready and gleaming. You have identified the facilitator and the scribe, and appointed any other roles you require (perhaps a time keeper). You have just finished reviewing the mission, vision and values that were created during the first set of meetings. You have explained the rules of the road, or allowed the team to establish how it will behave and you have documented these rules. There is energy in the room, and people are ready to roll. Your people are ready to come together to make the company better.

This is the moment when we take ahold of the principles and dictates of several different types of scientific process management theories and put them into practice. Your goal for this first meeting is to create a flow chart that describes a single process. The act of creating this flow chart will teach the team members how it's done. Choosing the most important process is not advised – in this case, learning how to create the process is more important than the outcome.

How to Define a Process

Start by volunteering, or asking the room to volunteer a process that they perform which is fairly simple. Expect to get a few suggestions that do not sound simple at all. Use this brainstorming opportunity as a way to establish how brainstorming is done, making sure that there is no conversation about the ideas generated at this stage, and no denigration of any suggestion.

For the purposes of this illustration, we will use the Reception Desk process as our starting point. This particular process comes up fairly often as the starting point of process improvement sessions. On the one hand, it sounds like a great process to use because it's a contained area that is limited to one person's job (in most cases), so it seems simple.

On the other hand, there's the issue that it's not a process. It is a role. Reception Desk is a role or function. Answering the Phone is a process. The difference can be thought of in parts of speech (noun oriented versus verb oriented). Alert your team to the difference, and then narrow in on a very simple aspect of reception, such as Answering the Phone.

Defining the Workflow

Hopefully, someone who fills the role or function of reception is represented at the meeting and can dictate exactly the steps they take to Answer the Phone. List them out on the visual board.

Note: If, for whatever reason, the person who is most knowledgeable about the workflow is not available, your team can still take a stab at outlining the workflow. It is, however, critical that the guesses made by the team are clearly marked DRAFT and that the person with the most information is interviewed to get the real information needed. If the team happened to get it right, great. If not, the process workflow can be updated before it is published.

Your list may take the shape of a bulleted list. That is fine. It is probably easier to edit as you go. For that accounting firm we keep talking about, your list might look something like this:

- Phone rings
- Pick up receiver
- Say the company greeting
- Listen to caller request
- Take a message or transfer call
- Hang up

And ultimately, it would translate into a flow chart that looks like this:

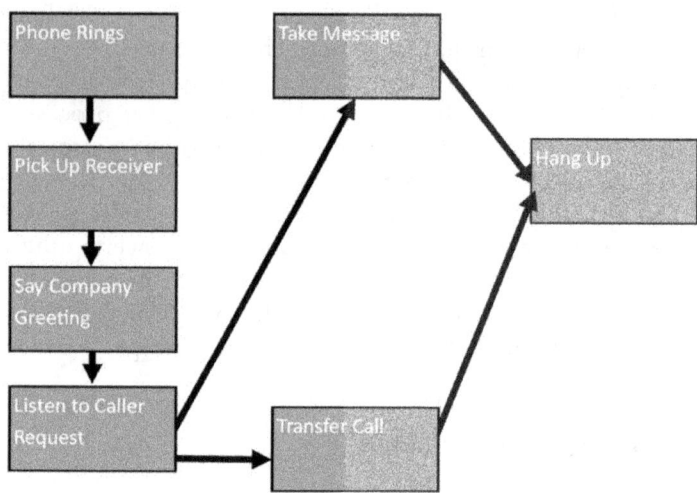

Note: There are a great many different software products that can be used in constructing flow charts. Some of them to simplify the process of creating and modifying charts, but they are not necessary to the process at all.

The "OR" statement in the process turns into a branch on the flow chart, because the flow can go either way.

The Answer the Phone process is such a great one to start with because almost everyone misses a critical point. If your team can spot it, you are in for a great process improvement cycle! Overlooking what is to be done if the caller leaves a message is one of the more common things that happens in this example. According to the flow chart, the message never goes anywhere – it stays with the receptionist. And this is the crux of a process improvement cycle. Properly defining what actually happens throughout the service provided is one of the hardest things to do, because we tend to skip steps and take things for granted.

The updated flow chart should look something like this:

PROCESS IMPROVEMENT FOR SERVICE BUSINESSES

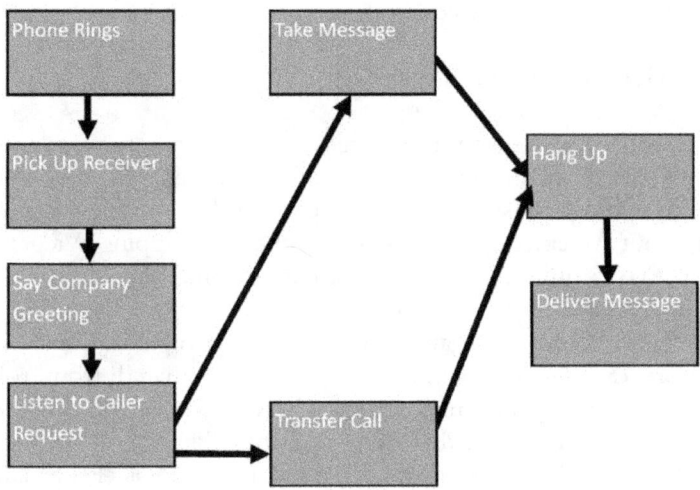

Having achieved a completed flow chart, your team deserves a break. It might be that this is the proper place to end your first meeting. It might be that your team is offsite on a retreat, and time is of the essence. Either way, take a little break to ensure that the concepts just reviewed can sink in for everyone. Use the time to create reproductions of the Team Rules and the flow chart for distribution.

Identifying Business Processes

Believe it or not, this is the worst moment possible to jump into flow chart madness. Rather, take a step back and create a list of the business processes that need to be defined. Following the Answer the Phone exercise, most team members will get the basics of the desired outcome and will come up with great suggestions. For those who might instinctively rebel against the idea of writing down "how everybody has to do everything" or "putting the job down in a binder," there can be satisfaction in knowing that this is a living document that will constantly be updated for the benefit of the whole organization, and that the documentation will be circulated throughout the entire organization for comment before it's finalized. Since this sense of malcontent usually arises from a sense of insecurity, the concepts of transparency and thoroughness and care are all helpful to express.

Service Versus Manufacturing

If you were performing this workflowing process at a manufacturing organization, you would be creating a list that would reference things present in the physical world. You would have an item about Assembling Widget A and one for Shipping Widgets A and B. Your flow charts would resemble something that is very real, and very easily seen in action.

Because you are operating inside a service organization, it can be more difficult to see processes as differentiated from roles. After all, if Bessy in Cube 10 has always done all of the client billing, isn't it true to say that Bessy *is* client billing?

Actually, it should be terrifying to say that Bessy is client billing. First it should scare the pants off of Bessy, because if she *is* client billing, she will never, ever be able to rise *above* client billing. Her tenure with the company is limited because of her competence, and that is not a value that most companies want to impress upon the staff.

It should also be frightening for the company's leadership. If the company has to equate a specific person with a process, it's likely that the organization is out of touch with how things are done. A reliable, long term employee who has invested a great deal in a process will be loath to change that process. Breaking this cycle before it begins is far easier, and requires documentation of the process with Bessy's cooperating.

See Appendix 1 for some legitimate processes which Service Organizations often discover during brainstorming. Appendix 2 outlines roles which are commonly found in Service Organizations.

Prioritization

You'll likely generate a disturbing number of processes that help your company to operate properly! There will be many that are entirely legitimate to document. There will be some that disappear into other processes as you continue through the assessment. In order for the project to remain manageable, determine with the team which three of the processes are the biggest picture processes.

Which projects touch the most people? Are there any of the processes that can be deemed absolutely core to the business? Selecting three processes, no matter how you determine the prioritization, will help the team stay focused. There may be the trend for a conversation about one process to diverge into other ideas about tangential processes. Having a board that outlines everything to come allows the team to make notes for later, without spinning out of control.

7 THE SCHEDULE

The process of process improvement takes some time. There are meetings, breakouts, flow charts to develop, and regular work day emergencies to handle. There is a great deal of time management that will help the process improvement process actually progress, thereby meaningfully improving the business.

The leaders on the team should be paying close attention to all team members, in connection with divisional management, to ensure that people on the team are able to get their regular work done. There should be a framework of trust and openness so that the process improvement team members can reach out to leaders on the team with any concerns, but the most highly performing members of the workforce are liable to fall prey to the trap of taking on too much. Keeping an eye out for critical deadlines that are on the calendar takes a little planning and some extra communication. It's a great way to exercise the skills that keep processes flowing in an organization!

Setting the Schedule

No matter if you keep your team calendar on an electronic shared calendar (probably the easiest way to circulate this information) or on a large calendar posted in a public office location, it is critical that the members of the process improvement team have ready access to the scheduled team events, deadlines, projected milestones and deliverable due dates. It can also be helpful if they can see cross-departmental deadlines for regular work, so they understand where their teammates are in their own processes. In this way they can plan their work deliverables around the demands of the team.

In addition, the team leadership can structure the meetings and demands of the team's service around known workload delivery dates. There is a need for consideration in time management, and it has to go both ways. The team leadership, in addition to watching out for those team members who may be suffering from overload, can structure the calendar to ease demands as needed, balance workloads among the resources available, and determine priorities for the organization as a while with a clear view into what is happening when.

This is the key to time management - to see the value of every moment.

-Menachem Mendel Schneerson

Creating and Communicating the Timelines

In the process of going through the process improvement process, there will be opportunities to set times for speakers during meetings, to create deadlines for sub-teams, and to generally describe the work to be done in terms of time. Time management is not something that comes naturally to some people. Even the most brilliant workers sometimes struggle to deal with time management. In fact, the most productive and talented workers are sometimes those who struggle the most. They are willing to put in long hours, work and learn extensively and volunteer time. While these habits might make an amazing work product, they do not a time manager make.

Leading by example, it is easy to illustrate principles of strong time management. For instance, set a cultural example on the team that meetings start on time. Call out those who absent themselves from team meetings, or who arrive late to meetings. You could even start a policy that the late arrivals must bring snacks to the next meeting. Stay away from "punishments" that involve taking on administrative work, or voluntelling late arrivers to take on more responsibilities for the team. This can lead to a lack of team performance due to resentment, something that buying cookies rarely generates.

Allowing people to see the beauty of a predictable workflow that leaves time for unpredictable life to happen is something of a gift. If you'd like to take the time out of your process improvement schedule to go through a top to bottom time management training, by all means, do it. However, if you have pressing matters relying upon the process review, you will need to demonstrate the way to a clear calendar.

Here are some strategies to use in this endeavor.

1. At the beginning of each meeting, distribute an agenda with clear timeframes for each topic on the agenda. Appoint a timekeeper who will count down the segments of the meeting as needed.
2. On the agenda, schedule breaks into the meeting. This can help not only control the cadence of the meeting itself, but constrain the group dynamics from getting out of hand.
3. Show up for every meeting. You undoubtedly have a busy schedule. You are undertaking a very important commitment for your business, and it takes precedence just as any other important business endeavor would. Do not be late. If you cannot avoid being late, follow the team rules and make appropriate restitution for wasting your teammates' time.
4. Outline the deliverables and when they are due as soon as you know they exist. Do not TBD or delay making deadlines until the picture becomes clearer, or you are further along in the process. This is not only courteous, but is also smart time management.
5. If your organization has a habit of assigning overlapping

work, cut it out. Assign the project to two people, or assign it to one person, but respect everyone's time sufficiently to expect a quality work product generated from excellent direction.
6. Enjoy the knowledge that enforcing the mores of time management will seep into the organization. If demonstrated properly, there will be ample opportunity to reap the rewards in the everyday life of the business.

Employing Flexibility

If the idea of a strict and enforced time management culture within the process improvement team sounds harsh, outside of the company's norms and against your management style, you will be happy to hear that employing flexibility within the team is at least equally important.

There will be times when emergency work flow issues will demand attention away from the team's goals. It is unavoidable that there will be conflicting priorities at some point. Your teammates can feel pulled in multiple directions when this happens, or forced into working hours which detract from family life and self-care. As a manager, it is critical that you place the care of your team as your primary focus. When you sense that team members are becoming over strained, it is important that you build some flexibility into the schedule. This embraces a key principle of the scientific process management platform called KANBAN. In this methodology, there is a defined process for controlling the flow of work so that it becomes neither overwhelming nor too slow to maintain output. The process is called buffering, and involves adding a floating point ahead of any work that could overwhelm the personnel performing the work. This buffer essentially provides the space needed to slow the roll of work into the team. It can also provide an opportunity to add a step which is skipped or missed due to work flow, like quality control.

As you develop the schedule of deliverables with your team, be prepared to build in buffers as needed. In fact, it is wise to build them in as you go. Your team may not understand at the beginning why deadlines are longer than they strictly need. You can rest assured that they will enjoy the space when it comes time to execute on multiple, conflicting demands.

Also rest assured that whatever buffers you build into your schedule will not be sufficient, or will be incorrectly placed. Repeat after me: part of the beauty of life is its unpredictability. When it comes to pass that something appears in the road and you need to swerve, the opportunity is there for you to demonstrate flexibility and perspective for the team.

Determining when to employ flexibility is one of the arts of management. Some choices have immediately obvious decisions. When it comes to choices between delaying work product or caring for your employees, there is no real choice. The decision must be caring for employees. Some choices have less obvious decisions, or have multiple potential waterfall effects. Some managers are hesitant to take decisions that are more complicated when in a public forum, such as a team meeting. The process improvement process would ask the manager to explore her decision-making thinking in the view of the team. In this way transparency is maintained, the trust of the team is preserved and your team has an opportunity to learn something.

Cost Analysis

Deciding what the best course of action is can be stressful when there are complex forces at work. Standing in the middle of two competing options when you have to make a quick call can often involve bringing in new or additional resources. This can mean temporary employees, additional consultants, outsourcing where possible, and potentially other resource adjustments. Bearing in mind that it is possible for resource allocation to be required during the process improvement cycle, it is wise to budget a certain amount of financial buffer to be utilized when needed, as you go through the process.

In addition, it is critical that there is a budget to implement changes required by the process. Some of those might be technological systems that are new to the company, or enhancements to the old systems. There can also be the need to hire new talent, as illuminated by process. In fact, the business's budget should allow for a great deal of leeway in the first year of process improvement as a variety of different outcomes can shift the need for spend.

Flexibility is one of the great assets in business. Between managing time and managing financial assets, creating appropriate personnel allocations and driving the business needs forward, flexibility has to be one your greatest assets.

Accountability and Deadlines

This chapter has been centered around the need to strategize time and other resources in order to bolster the business. Those resources are scarce. You are dedicating your treasure and your army to the goal of capturing more land, of increasing your share. In order for that dedication of resources to matter, your seriousness and your expectation of success must both be communicated to the organization.

Unfortunately, the way that human beings generally work, giving one heart-felt speech to the masses at the beginning of the process improvement cycle will not make the point sufficiently. You will need to be in communication with the management, supervisors and the floor as the process progresses. You will need to ensure that the principles you are attempting to formalize in the process improvement cycle – in fact, by beginning the process improvement cycle – should be exercised as early as possible.

You, your team, and all of your employees, need to be held accountable in order to actualize the benefits of the process improvement investment. A process is, but nature, a statement of accountability. Following the process will lead to the desired results. Ergo, following the process is something to which all employees are accountable. However, sometimes following the process is difficult. There are ethical considerations: is following the process the right thing to do? There are business considerations: is following the process the most profitable thing to do? There are customer considerations: is following the process the best thing for the relationship?

The commitment that leadership makes when undertaking a scientific process improvement strategy is that the results of the improvement cycle will be honored. There will not be exceptions and overrides that frivolously devalue the standard. It is, first, because exceptions to the rule are costly in terms of time and quality and dollars. It is also, second, because the trust of your team in the process they design is upheld only by the sanctity of the process that you create. And, third, it is because of the trust in your leadership which you want your team to hold. Without any of those items, the process improvement cycle is merely an exercise and unimportant.

Upholding the trust of your team can be one result of a well-constructed process. The process, and its regular and transparent enforcement, acts as a covenant between you, the leader, and the team mate on the ground each day. Capturing the trust of your team mates is valuable, and can be done by honoring the results of the process development cycle as though they were the only decision tree possible.

Finishing the Product

The time will come when the process is defined. It may seem as though it is an unreachable goal, forever far in the distance, but completing a process definition is something that will happen. We have reviewed the necessity of taking the process as gospel. It is also necessary to circulate the completed process to the employees on the floor.

Some organizations undertake this as an educational opportunity. Retraining and testing on the process can help employees learn it quickly, and when proper incentives are attached to the implementation of the process, it is quickly reinforced behavior.

Some organizations keep it simple, and publish the finished product for review. Still others are content to allow the management at the middle levels explain the new processes, how they will be interpreted, and what opportunities they afford to the staff.

All of these are options, depending on the status of the organization and its culture. It may seem odd to include this section under the heading of "Scheduling", but there is method to the madness. There are two reasons this summary of process release and adoption is included here in the Scheduling section. For one thing, the need to explain and possibly train on new processes should take into consideration the company's workload and inbound work, and should ensure that the right resources are available on hand in order to execute the release. It is incredibly likely that some stumbling will occur during the rollout of the new process, and having the leeway to deal with that is helpful.

Workload considerations can be managed with buffers, or with additional resources. Resources of this nature might include temporary workers, or it might be is that there are internal resources that can be allocated to high-work-density teams. It is only possible to know what the time constrictors are at the team level if there is documentation of where the workload stands at any given point. Using an electronic work calendar, task assignments, a CRM or other tools to ensure that scheduling on the floor allows for the education on and adoption of the plan will help.

Additional considerations are the resources needed to properly schedule the adoption cycle. A finished product is just a static document until it is published. Assistance in handling the day to day matters of the firm, while also introducing a new and refined way of working, is one of the biggest resource constraints in the world today. At the outset of the process, or perhaps when you have your first chart to share with middle management, consider the idea of a company workflow engine that can be shared via a calendar view.

8 COMMUNICATION

Throughout this book you have gotten a sense of how important communication is to the accurate and healthy adoption of your workflow process. Without clear communication during the process building cycle, the workflows produced will be less than useless. Without clear communication from management, the staff will not know what to do to adopt the workflow. Without clear communication from the staff, the process improvement team will not know what to adapt in the workflows to gain further efficiency. Open, clear and transparent communication creates a feedback loop that is very necessary to a scientific process management scheme. Without it, there is no hope of the workflow doing its job.

The workflows themselves act as a basic communication tool. They are a streamlined representation of what happens in your organization on a daily basis. When some people communicate about process, it is much easier for them to have a flow chart to point at, so that they can logically construct their thoughts. Other people are more at home reading paragraphs, and would like to see the flow charts translated into a written explanation. This is perfectly acceptable, but the written explanation cannot take the place of the flow charts; you can simply produce both documents.

Some leaders are better communicators than others. There are plenty of ways to improve your communication skills, if you feel they might be a weakness. Another option is to appoint a chief communicator for the process improvement team. This person will act as the process improvement team's Public Relations engine, getting the correct information about the workflow cycle, the process improvement team and the adoption process out into the open. This role is critically important, as you will see.

Setting Team Communication Expectations

Communication is the heart of the process improvement exercise. From the very beginning, when your visual board is ready to receive brainstorming information from the team, you are setting rules and norms about communication. You are showing your team, and the organization as a whole, what to do. When you say that there is no wrong idea in brainstorming, you allow for transparency and safe communication. Setting this expectation is a covenant with your employees.

Just like you did with scheduling, it is important to set the expectations and mores for the process improvement team's communication structure. It is recommended that, if possible, the communication about the team's work be documented so that everyone can access it. For this reason, some experts demand that only during the process improvement meetings should conversation about the workflows take place. In today's geographically distributed environment, and with the business pressures that companies often face, this may not be practical. Particularly for distributed teams, it may not be worthwhile.

Alternatives include arranging for ad hoc discussions in a way that uses modern technology. For instance, you might use a bulletin board web site to allow everyone to comment, discuss, and otherwise toss around ideas. You could set up a mobile app that the team can share. You could even use a simple email distribution group. It is recommended that, no matter what method you choose, you make it clear to your team that team communications are "all or none" – there should be no conversations that include only a few members of the team.

Note: Very occasionally, something may come up that is so sensitive that it must be discussed one-on-one. The point of this segment is not to ban appropriate communication in the workplace, but to maintain the group nature of the workflow discussions.

Other communications pitfalls inside the process improvement team can be handled, as well. There should be the expectation of courteous and reasoned communication at all times. Hopefully this expectation is already engrained in your company's culture. If you see that this is not the case, taking a moment to establish the expectation as part of your Values exercise can be a worthwhile step.

You may also want to take some logistics steps around communication as your workflow nears completion. How often are sub-teams required to report in? What about near the end of the process, how often will the draft documents be sent around for review, and by what method? These are not plans that need to be set in stone when you begin, but be aware that they are going to arise later in the process.

Setting Organizational Communication Expectations

As much as your team members are going to be seen as leaders in the organization, it is important to establish for them what to expect in their own home workgroups. There is an option to distribute a team memo on this, which saves time, and a sample is included in Appendix 3. In an organization where trust and communication have been badly damaged, though, there should be a frank and head-on conversation about new approaches during one of the first process improvement team meetings.

Communicating about communication can be difficult. You may not even be sure that there is a communication problem in your company, and if you suspect there might be, you may not be sure how to ask about its depth. For some leaders, asking the team to describe ways in which communication has failed them turns quickly into a blame game, and that is not productive. In fact, it can be toxic as it introduces the concepts of individualism and personality into the conversation, which is supposed to be about workflows and process.

In many service companies, however, the workflow lends itself to illuminating communication gaps. Where the manufacturing process will show logical breaks in the chain of production (how things move), the service company's flow chart will often illuminate areas where information does not properly flow from one person to another, or is unacknowledged when it does make the journey.

Locating a workflow in which there is a lot of back and forth, or in which several people need to sign off on a project before it moves forward, is a great way to bring up this topic of communication in general, and to allow the conversation to gracefully digress if it needs to.

Determining the state of the communication norms in the organization is an important step, and it can lead to a better, stronger work product from the process improvement team.

Scheduling is Communicating

Besides being helpful in its own right, scheduling is communication. It tells someone what is expected and when. It also gives some subtle communication queues that you want to harness for the benefit of the team.

For instance, if you create a breakout team of four people who are to write up the workflow for the process of Sending Invoices to Customers, you will set up a series of deliverables for that sub-team. You will then put those deliverables on their due dates on the team calendar, so that everyone can see when things are coming due.

If you then create another sub-team that is asked to investigate and revise the completed Distribute the Snail Mail process, you may expect (and your process improvement team as a whole may agree) that they will need less time to complete their assignment. However, if you assign then shorter dates for completing their work, they may feel slighted or resentful. The optics of time management are greatly enhanced with the addition of the work calendar discussed in the previous section. Not only does the layout of deliverable dates which cannot be moved and the overlay of process improvement team obligations create an objective framework by which the team can establish the right work completion timeframes, it is a great way to explore the workflow concepts of scientific process management and other frameworks.

In other words, scheduling is a communication device that can be read by some as a subtle challenge or as an endorsement. Removing that filter by creating an objective scheduling mechanism is one of the ways to clear the communication field and add transparency.

There are, of course, other areas of communication that carry subtle and potentially detrimental tones which may not ring for some, but can toll loudly for others. This is why the improvement cycle recommends sticking to objective times to move meetings forward, to starting on time, no matter what or who is running late, and other objective stances regarding time.

Be aware of statements that could potentially exclude or denigrate a department, their efforts or a manager. Stick with the framework of not commenting on a person, but rather on a process. Removing names from the workflow allows the conversation to be about the function, or role, rather than about who's performing it.

Normalizing Communication

You may be thinking that this is all very well and good, and even logical, but it will feel stilted and disingenuous. If your organization has a different cultural norm, you are probably correct. Initially, the use of a communication framework will feel very odd, and your employees may regard it with suspicion. It is a great time to reach into the organization at a deep level and help people train on your communication strategy.

Communication training can take different forms. There are many organizations now offering forms of communication training, such as anger management or sexual harassment training, via the web. There are opportunities to do in-house training by management for each team. This is one area in which you may benefit significantly from bringing in a professional coach. Simply put, if your company has a history of communication issues, it is going to be easier for someone standing outside of the system to pinpoint and remedy those issues. Seen as an objective outsider, there will be less resentment from the staff at the presentation of new rules and expectations.

In addition, the right consultant can be an advocate for change throughout the organization. When your process improvement team is called upon to disseminate information, the communications expert can work with the PR Coordinator to create talking points, smooth and temper the message, and generate a simple and effective communication strategy for the whole project. In fact, some consultants would be willing to work as your team's PR Coordinator. One word of caution on that: you will be taking complicated ideas and turning them into simple statements. It is recommended that the person liaising with the consultant be fully versed in what the team is doing, as a member of the team, so that the core information being communicated is accurate.

Determining the right coach can seem like an additional daunting project in the midst of several daunting projects. It does take some time to find a great coach. For this reason, it is recommended that you begin interviewing communications consultants or coaches before you launch the process improvement cycle. In Appendix 4 you will find an order of operations which will prepare the organization for the process improvement cycle, and approximately when they should be undertaken.

Multichannel Communication

It's no secret people take in information differently. There are those who are more visual, some who like to hear information, and some who are kinesthetic. Structuring your process improvement team's communication structure as recommended will give the team ample opportunity to use all communication methods, thus giving every member of the team the chance to experience information at their best. In addition, carrying the idea of multichannel communication through to the organization is something that will help to bring the company up a level, regardless of the process improvement cycle.

To review, the recommended communication strategies for the process improvement team are:

1. Visual Board
2. Verbal Expression and Discussion
3. Graphical Workflow
4. Paragraph Format Workflow
5. Documented Post-meeting

The visual board is the most useful to the most people, as the majority identify with the visual learning style. The second most common is the verbal expression, which will be getting plenty of air time during the team's meetings. For those who appreciate information more when they can touch it, or write it down, there is a special role on the team: that of the scribe. If you can identify those team members who are best able to absorb knowledge when they are hands-on, offer them the role of scribe. The opportunity to put the data up on the visual board will allow them to best engage with the team and make the strongest contributions.

The communication strategy of ensuring conversations are fully documented when they happen outside of the team meetings will benefit everyone, since information which is completely absent is not useful. When verbal conversations happen between only two people on a large team, a team of twelve has lost the data that was exchanged.

Security In Communication

Your team is going to be discussing the plot points that make your organization a best seller. In fact, because you are a service organization, these points are even more critically unique than they would be in a manufacturing scenario.

For instance, consider these two workflows, both of which describe the creation of a company's primary product.

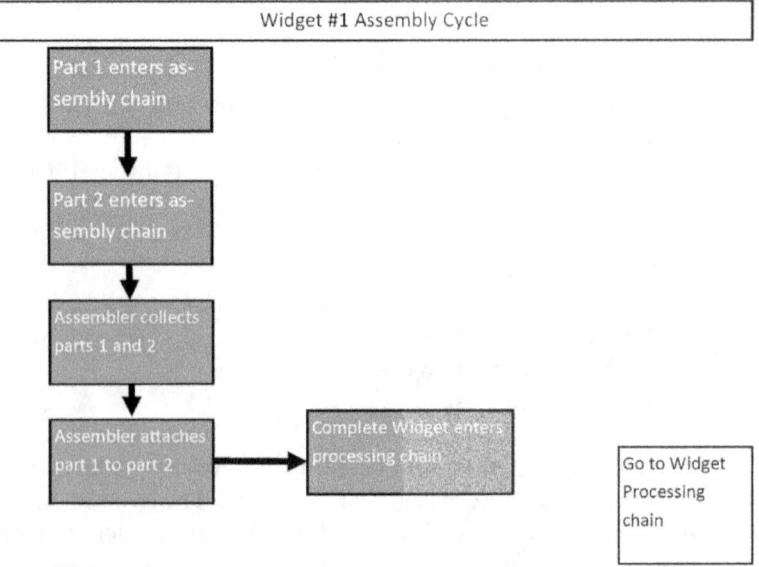

PROCESS IMPROVEMENT FOR SERVICE BUSINESSES

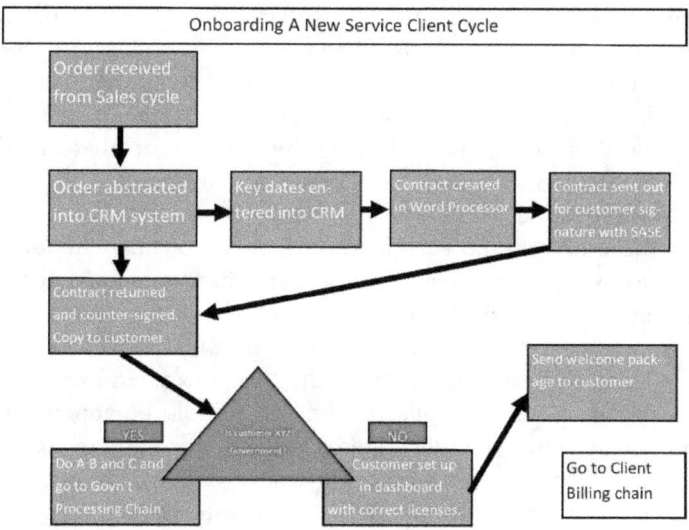

While the manufacturing workflow focuses on the assembly of a product, with limited additional information presented, the service workflow offers up an entire strategy about the company's clients and their requirements. This information is core to your business's success and should be protected.

Smaller organizations or those in the start-up phase may not utilize things like confidentiality agreements. If that works for your company, there is no need to make a change. However, there is the need to secure the conversations which happen inside the process improvement team in order to protect the overall business mission. This may seem to fit awkwardly within the overarching conversation about transparency and trust. The security bubble you need to impose, however, is something that should arch over the entire organization, not just the process improvement team.

For instance, when your team develops the workflow for the production of that key service, your process improvement team does not need to withhold information from the other employees. However, all employees should know instinctively not to discuss that workflow outside of the organization. If you are going to utilize the services of a communications consultant, this could be a great topic to embrace before the process improvement cycle even begins.

Some service organizations, particularly those that work with the government or are regulated industries, are subject to some very specific regulations about what they can and cannot discuss, with whom, and how. These regulations are key to an organization's success, and following them can mean that the idea of embracing "transparency" in operational communications is not going to be possible.

For these organizations, it is important to consider the idea of information security and privacy as a hierarchical structure. If there is data (including workflow process data) which can only be seen by those with a Top Secret clearance, or by those who work on a specific team, that data should be clearly tagged and an explanation of the regulation which applies to the data should be appended to the information. In many file systems and structures, there are ways to use "tags" or "classifications" to denote files which should be private to a specific group. When the information is tagged appropriately, and tag is attached that calls out the regulation securing the information, that qualifies as transparency. The employees without the rights to the data are getting as much information as they can get about the information.

When a service company with restrictions such as these is going through the process improvement cycle, there may be business processes that have to be reviewed by a small sub-team with appropriate clearance, and then published only to the teams with the rights to the information. This, again, is acceptable inasmuch as the reason for the restriction is called out along with a tag about the restricted status.

If a review of your internal information controls seems to be in the cards, consider undertaking that review after the completion of the process improvement cycle. During the cycle, there may be some discoveries about what information is needed and what can be released that would cause a re-do of work completed if the review is undertaken before the process starts.

Communicating Throughout the Organization

The game of telephone doesn't seem to resonate now that everyone has text messaging. In Telephone, a person whispers a statement to the next person in line. That person delivers the message to the next person, and so on. Most of the time, when the message reaches the end of the chain, it will differ in some significant ways from the original whisper. Often these differences are hilarious in the game, but when it comes to your company, flaws in the chain of communication are not funny at all.

Miscommunication is one of the most significant ways in which a company can fail itself. The opportunities for miscommunication are many, and they can come up anywhere. When you are dealing with something as critical as your business's operating processes and procedures, it is important that there are no miscommunications. In part, the flow charting will help eliminate any discontinuity or assumptions. This is important, but the work of communicating clearly does not end there.

In addition to miscommunication, there can be gaps in communication flow that can leave a department or a key individual out of the information flow. These gaps can result in rework, frustration and employee disenchantment. It is pretty easy to skip over communication gaps during the flow charting process. After all, it can be difficult to prove a negative and highlight something that is not there. One trick to stop the gaps is to ask the workflow design team what is missing in each flow chart. What is not there on the page that should be? If the team does not catch a gap during their process, the odds are that the impacted parties will catch it when the flow charts are published. Take commentary from the field on how to improve the flow charts seriously. Even if the input is not incorporated into the work flow, there may be the seed of an idea there that could be used in a different way.

Since that is the case, put your process improvement team on "ears open" mode throughout the workflow process, and after the work flows are published. As you will see in subsequent sections, there will be plenty of time after the publication to review and revise the workflows. Continue to utilize the communications norms and systems that have been established after the team completes the publication of the first workflow drafts.

Diffusing Communication Conflicts

A word about maintaining transparency and trust on the team, and indeed throughout the organization, when communication conflicts show up. And it is very likely that they will show up.

When one person or group feels that they have been misunderstood, it is natural for them to feel urgency about correcting the situation. That urgency can translate in a variety of ways that can further hinder clear communication. By providing a way for communication to be documented, there is a simple and straightforward way for misunderstandings to be made clear.

In the event that a communication error causes hurt feelings or personal response, the situation can escalate quickly. If this happens within a small organization or within a process improvement team, the trust that is required for success can be damaged. To rescue the situation, a leader with trust is needed to re-connect the parties, clear up the communication error, and provide a demonstration of how to handle such issues in the future.

The task of a leader in a safe and transparent organization is to build a framework in which employees throughout the organization can confidently say, "I'm sorry. I think we had a misunderstanding," and expect an outcome that is mature, sensible, and moves the company forward. This project epitomizes cultural change. A communications consultant can help lay the groundwork for this endeavor, and provide pointers which can help senior management actualize that open door policy everyone talks about, but in the end, this is something that takes practice.

Non-Verbal Communication

It appears that, as human beings, we receive almost 80% of input through non-verbal cues. This is disconcerting when over 100% of verbal communication is done through verbal cues. When you stop to consider how much work goes into crafting just the right word choice to communicate a message, and then realize that only 10% of the data is getting through because your hands are clenched and your hair is a bit messy, you can get truly discouraged.

Help your company's leaders deal with non-verbal communication cues. They may have ticks or tells which may be sending the wrong message. They may close themselves off due to insecurity or sensitivity. Some managers may feel challenged by particular employees. A communications coach can work with leaders one-on-one to improve their non-verbal communication style. Some will also evaluate the posture of the organization as a whole or a team when in a meeting situation, which can be valuable if you have a unit that is not performing to spec and you cannot figure out what is holding them back. Since so much unconscious information is displayed non-verbally, it is very worthwhile to gather the information when possible. Some employees may not even be aware of what they are communicating with they cross their arms and legs and roll their eyes.

KATHLEEN HURLEY

9 THE CONCEPT OF FAIL

The world, if you look at it from a rather negative but realistic point of view, is full of failure. If you live in a city and take public transportation, the late arrival of your train or bus is a failure. If you are grocery shopping and there is a shortage of a critical item to your diet, like bread, that is a failure. If you are accustomed to driving one way on a street, but that street is closed without any warning, that is a failure.

Failure is something that many human beings are hardwired to experience as frustrating, limiting and shameful. When the failure is due to a personal action, it can be a devastating experience. The less accustomed to experiencing failure a person is, the more devastating the experience of it can be. What constitutes a legitimate failure to one person may not register as failure to another, while the sense of being shamed by a failure may flare more greatly in one person than in another.

In short, failure is an intensely personal experience, but one that is encountered by almost every person on the planet in some form or another on a daily, if not hourly, basis. A leader in an organization is sometimes seen as the Chief Failure Identifier, seeking out issues with personnel and systems and bringing them to the attention of the responsible party. Bringing them to the attention of the responsible party sometimes takes the form of a disciplinary action, as the failure is clearly the result of the negligence of oversight of a person in charge. Sometimes the form is more subtle, and is communicated through various layers of passive-aggressive political or financial manipulation.

Studies have shown that these less overt methods of leadership communication are not useful or efficient. Probably it did not require studies to show this – it is common sense that less direct action will lead to a less accountable result. It is common sense that there is little benefit in blaming someone on the first go for an issue they were unaware of to begin with, an approach which will only cause resentment.

Some organizations attempt to quantify failure by imposing systems upon the production process. Quality control, a concept which is part of organizations that embrace all manner of management philosophies, is a result of the idea that things will inevitably be done or handled incorrectly. A quality control process attempts to capture the errors before they enter the distribution system, keeping the quality of the product high for the consumer. In a manufacturing system, quality control is critical to everything from the perception of the brand to the actual sale of goods. Proactive management of the failed product results in less waste, less time spent and less cost to the organization.

In a service organization, quality control can seem a little more complicated to impose. After all, there is often not a physical good to be inspected. Some service companies have a tradition or a philosophy of responding to consumer complaints with a swiftness, reactively imposing a quality control process on the back end. This is a difficult system to manage objectively, since customer complaints are generally made by human beings, and people are often less than objective.

When managing a service organization, the ability to define a process brings an unprecedented ability to control for quality. Not only will your process define what is the correct (and thus acceptable) means of achieving success, but it will also identify where in the process certain actions are to take place. Since order of operations is as important in a service industry as it is in a manufacturing industry, there is a significant level of control imposed when there is a defined process which can be followed.

When A Process Failure Happens

When a defined process exists, and failure still occurs, it can be surprising to the leadership. After all the time, energy and money dedicated to bringing the process into being, not to mention the training and communication that have gone into creating a cultural shift, it can also cause anger, fuel blame and inspire a search for a scapegoat. While these are natural human emotional responses to a shock or betrayal of expectations, they are not useful emotions to resolving a misunderstanding.

This is truly where the rubber of all that has been explored in this book meets the road. The need for strong communication has never been more intense than when a process failure occurs. The framework of the process improvement team's norms and mores can support the deductive thought needed to fix the process. The management education that has taken place can only help the employees involved improve their understanding. In short, the old style of "management by walking around," which seeks to identify *who* is operating how and when, is replaced by a management of process, which seeks to improve *what* is done, and which trickles through the entire organization seamlessly.

Most scientific process improvement systems are centered around the idea of failure. They exist to minimize and diffuse the potential for a failed execution. When a process improvement cycle is undertaken, it is sometimes because a company is repeatedly hitting the same failure point. Sometimes it is because a failure point hit once was so impactful that it damaged the brand. And other times, it is because there is a need to tighten up on systemic waste, or demonstrate a need for additional resources, or improve the flow of information through the organization – all small failures that could add up to a big fail.

An attempted response to a failure must be established by the process improvement cycle itself. When there is a built-in check that is not balanced, the workflow should not move on. These checks are necessary to the seamless execution of process, and a limitation of re-work.

When it becomes clear that a defined process does not include all of the checks and balances that it should, the workflow must be updated. The failure of the workflow to stop and check at important junctures can be significant. After completing the design of the workflow, ensure that the team reviews the charts together to add in any balances that are needed. This can reduce the overall perception that the workflow fails, and can improve the product that is experienced by customers at the end of the day.

The Process, Not the Person

There is a commonality that is often cited as a weakness in scientific process management, summed up in the phrase, "It's the process, not the person."

When this phrase specifically came into being, it was seen as revolutionary. The old ideas about eliminating a problem worker and bringing the company into a new level of productivity and efficiency (a methodology which often caused more problems than it solved) were thrown out the window. As long as the individuals in the organization were accurately and accountably following the process, they could not be at fault for weaknesses or failures in production. The process would be continually refined and revised, adding new advances in knowledge and technology to the workflow, initiating a cycle of continuous improvement for the company.

There was a slight miscommunication at some point in the introduction of the "process, not person" concept. Some managers took the theory to mean that a person could *never* be at fault any longer, and that there was no room for or need of improvement at the workforce level. Criticisms surfaced that made it seem as though scientific process improvement systems were reducing workers to cogs in a giant wheel over which they had limited or no control, and into which they had no input.

In manufacturing and production, the cog in the wheel theory was acceptable to many. Repetitive processes are, in fact, not individualized. A person's style and personality are not relevant to many aspects of the manufacturing process.

However, in the world of service companies, the idea of the individual is paramount. Strong customer service depends upon the right person delivering the right message with the right personality. Effective sales and service delivery requires a personal brand and style that are somewhat rare and valuable. Even internal services, like accounting, require a person of specific talents and a serious ability to focus on detail. These are personality traits, not process elements as defined in many of the original iterations of scientific process management styles.

For this reason, many people assumed that the world of service organizations could not be served by scientific process improvement methodologies. Service organizations kept going along with the idea that the right people, brought together in the right positions at the right times, would produce the magic formula for success. There are stories that certainly prove this to be true. There are also stories of how this theory got some people into big trouble.

There is no reason to divorce the scientific process improvement cycle from the fact that human beings are executing the processes. In industries where people are required to be creative, cutting-edge and responsive to the needs of others, it can be even more helpful to have a defined process system. It not only helps the organization determine where it stands, but it helps the employees execute in their very best way.

How Process Improvement Can Influence and Improve Hiring

There is something to be said for the idea that the right combination of personalities will spark the magic that makes a company skyrocket. It is people, and the energy they produce when they come together with a common goal, that make a company great. Everything else is window dressing.

What constitutes the right personalities, though, and what exactly makes up that magic combination, may be very different from each person's unique perspective. Some people involved in the hiring process will look at the past success of an individual as an indicator of future performance and be satisfied with that analysis. Some people who are interviewing candidates will want to see the individual's stress responses when under pressure. Others will give precedence to the candidates personal statement about their own hopes and values.

All of those subjective criteria can be very important in hiring the right personality for a service organization's team. So are:
- A willingness to follow process
- The ability to think creativity
- An accountability for personal and team behaviors

- A desire to improve personally and professionally

Understanding the workflow that the candidate will be responsible for can add detail to the job description and candidate requirements that narrow the field of resumes presented for review, limit the noise of unnecessary interviews, and help to make the decision between the final contenders. There is a helpful hiring tool in Appendix 6 that can bring together your workflow design and your position requirements.

Opportunities for Coaching and Learning

The commitment management makes to respecting and embracing the workflow processes developed by the team means that there can be some real gains in employee relations and changes in management style. Generally, these changes impact an organization only for the good, as they open up communication. However, some managers can be phased by the requirement of more one on one time with their teams if they are unaccustomed to that way of handling business.

Particularly in an organization that has had a player-coach mentality (where managers are also production workers), there can be some tension among those who have been seen as the best managers. They may perceive that additional management overhead detracts from their productivity. There can also be some managers who decide that their team's well-being is threatened by the new process implementation, and respond to the sense of threat in their own manner. This can entail withdrawal, outright rebellion, or passive-aggressive or political maneuvers.

Because managers, particularly those who are highly respected in an organization, are leaders in their own right, there is a significant benefit to offering them first look at the workflow plan which is developed by the team. Since they will also be responsible for enforcing the plan, it is courteous to do so.

Presenting the workflow plan to the management team and de facto leaders in the company also offers you the opportunity to observe responses. Since offering coaching and training to management is going to be one of the most important needs you address between the time of plan completion and the time of roll out, you want this opportunity to identify issues before they arise.

If time is particularly short, or if you recognize the need for coaching in most of your leadership staff, bring in a consultant to set the stage, then arrange a mentoring program for the leaders.
Once you feel the leadership team is ready to embrace the process and to stand up to support the staff in their efforts, the next step is to release the plan to the staff.

Assuring the staff that their input in the process is valued, and making it clear that the system requires constant improvement, are the key messages to send during the rollout of your work product. Managers should expect to get feedback from their teams, and should have a means to pass that information to the process improvement team for review.

Accountability (redux)

When managers perceive a failure in the process, they may not know what to do natively about the issue. Their instinct to discipline the employee may not be appropriate, if the problem is due to a process issue. However, an employee who is not following process is going to require discipline.

Particularly in those smaller organizations, or organizations that are built on a matrix model, or those which are very horizontal, the idea of disciplining employees may exist, but can be a concept that is not often exercised. When personality and character traits drive the organization rather than workflow and process, it is tough to know when to sit an employee down and discuss a problem. Particularly when the company has responded reactively to complaints, rather than addressing issues of failure proactively, there can be a lack of formality in the employee management process.

Instituting a system by which managers can easily discuss concerns with employees is critical to the success of a scientific management system. The key theory to impart to management, and then to the staff, is that there are going to be situations when the process fails. In those cases, it is everyone's responsibility to bring the situation to management's attention quickly, and with recommendations for process revision. However, that does not that the process can be avoided, ignored and rejected. Like any relationship, the company's relationship to the process will experience ups and downs, and revisions and new perspectives will be necessary. This is part of the way continuous improvement works.

Employees should be clear on the fact that their adherence to process, and their participation in improving the organization, will be what they are judged upon. If they are not able to be accountable for their work in terms of the new workflow, they will be visiting Human Resources. This communication goes a long way toward disrupting the myth that scientific process management will not impact personnel decisions. In other words, it is not the "process over the person," but the person driving the process that is the most important thing in the organization.

10 RE VISION

When your workflow is complete it should reflect not only an accurate map of what your company does each day, but your vision for the company. If you sit back and look at the flow chart for Answering the Phone, does it do what you want it to? Does it reflect to callers the professionalism, warmth, tone and persona that you want people to gather about your company?

The workflow design produced should tie in, at all times and in all ways, with the mission and vision statements that you produced at the very beginning. The values that you stated should be supported by the way in which the company works. Where there is misalignment, revision will naturally occur as it is discovered, but revision should reflect alignment with the mission, vision and values, and not the other way around.

Making the work process line up with the mission statement of the company is often seen as a particularly ephemeral project by the more linear thinkers in the group. However, it is not difficult to take a review of the process structure to make sure it supports the needs of the mission statement.

Take this example of a mission statement:

Accounting Services Corp provides trustworthy and secure accounting services.

Do the workflow processes, as designed, ensure that the employees are working in a trustworthy manner? Are the processes structured so that the data produced by the employees is beyond question?

What about security – are the processes and systems aligned with best in class security measures?

Where there are gaps between the team's understanding of the mission statement and the process documents, filling them in is typically a structural exercise. Adding in quality assurance blocks and adjusting for additional checks and balances can go a long way toward assuring accuracy and security systems reviews can be done on a regular reoccurring basis. In this way, the mission statement (and values, and vision) can be supported by the every-day work of the workforce. Knowing that the movements of the process embody the vision of the organization adds gravitas to the process system, and increases adoption. As revisions take place, being careful to consistently re-align the workflow documentation with the company's fundamentals is key.

Constantly Revisiting the Design

As you have observed, the process improvement cycle, once adopted, is a constantly moving target. Technology, market forces, personnel recommendations and new customer requirements can all be forces that lead to revisions of the process documents your team has created. During the first calendar year following the release of the first draft of process, consider holding monthly meetings to go over input, review metrics and consider new buffers and checks that need to go into place. Determining the number of meetings is something that is best left up to the team, but structuring them so that they occur regularly can help maintain the norms that have already been established and continue to cultural shift that has begun in the organization.

Avoid the temptation to revise for the sake of revision, but be open to meaningful adjustments to the process. In some situations, revising the process will involve tearing it down and going through the whole cycle of review on that process again. This is acceptable at any stage of the release, even though it is an investment in time. In most organizations, one process touches another. Being certain to adapt linked workflows as one changes is important.

Measuring Success

It can be difficult to know how things are going under any management system. In an organization without distinct transparency as part of the culture, it can be even harder since people may be reluctant to comment freely upon their observations.

There are many up sides to implementing a scientific process improvement system. One of the biggest is the ability to measure outcomes. This is another area wherein process improvement for a service organization differs from that of a production organization. In a production framework, it is easy to count the number of widgets produced, or sold, and compare it to previous outputs. In a service organization, there are no widgets, and process improvement often focuses on overhead-bearing areas. The overhead-bearing departments in a company (sometimes called "back office support") are typically unprepared to collect data about their own productivity. In a small organization, it may seem particularly onerous to contemplate logging every activity done by every employee in the organization for the sole purpose of measuring their output. However, there are ways to measure the process's impact without imposing tracking systems on the employees.

The simplest way to measure the outcome of a process improvement is to compare it to the old process. Any process flow chart will include a number of boxes that describe steps in the workflow. When the number of steps is reduced, the workflow has been simplified. Therefore, additional efficiency has been gained.

Another measurement of a process's impact is the survey. Asking questions proactively of your customers, your employees and your stakeholders will give you the ability to act on information before it reaches a critical state, and will help close any feedback loops that might be in the process itself.

Finally, determining the outcome of the process improvement cycle can also be done in a subjective way. How is the mood in the company? What is morale like? How are teams working to improve their own processes, and what innovations are coming from the field? If these aspects of company participation have been limited in the past and now feel as though they are on the upswing, that in itself is a measurement of the success of the endeavor.

Making Use of the Process Improvement Document as A Guiding Document

There are many guiding documents in an organization, including legal documents, budgets and operating policies. The process improvement documentation should become part of the organization's guiding literature.

Because some departments or segments of the business were probably not addressed during the initial process improvement cycle, it is possible that those departments may not take the initiative to familiarize themselves with what the final work product. There are definite benefits to encouraging the understanding of the workflow throughout the entire company. Some of the areas of the back office, in particular, can utilize the document, even though it may not appear to directly impinge upon their work processes. Some examples follow.

Human Resources

As already discussed at some length, documenting the processes that the company values and follows can help in the hiring process. It can also lead to the improvement of employee relations, communication and the appropriate application of coaching and training.

When Human Resources has a complete understanding of what functions the organization requires, and why, there is a synergy that can be felt in the company. Where in some organizations HR is seen as a source of discipline or fear alone, the application of a scientific process management system can bring HR into tighter integration with the company.

One way to think about the entire over-arching process improvement cycle is in the context of proactive versus reactive. When HR is awaiting complaints or requests for help from managers, there is less opportunity for HR to grow employees, recruit winners and retain those in whom the company has heavily invested. When the expectations of the workforce are clearly outlined, the reactive nature of Human Resources shifts. Most HR professionals are excited by the opportunity to become more embedded in, and more functional with, the people they support.

Having Human Resources function as a valued ally of the entire company is one of the best ways to keep employees engaged and feeling valued. The aspects of learning management, retention and career management that HR can bring to the employee's day to day existence will only enhance their view that the company values their input and wants each member as part of the team.

Information Technology

IT professionals, be they inside your organization or part of an outsourced provider's staff, are going to be some of the biggest allies for process documentation and improvement. That might be at odds with some stereotypes about IT professionals, but the truth is that IT runs on best practices, processes that are documented and strict workflows. Without those underlying the IT field, there would be far more downtime and risk than there is today.

Programmers follow processes like Devops without thinking much about it. Networking professionals delve into troubleshooting using a variety of models that outline the most reliable way to solve problems the most quickly. Even the Help Desk profession has a guiding plan for delivering the correct information to the correct people, while giving excellence in customer service.

What some Information Technology service providers, and even internal players, fail to address is the innovation aspect of IT. In some industries, IT spend is so limited that the pros may not feel as though they have the leeway to recommend sweeping change unless it's also cost saving. Some IT professionals are just not trained to be creative, strategic thinkers. No matter what the reason, innovation may not be coming from IT, and that is a major suppressor to growth and efficiency inside a small to mid-sized company.

With the illustration of company processes in a quantifiable document, there should be ample opportunity for IT to present strategies, systems and software that could reduce the number of steps required in almost every area of a service business.

If the strategic design is not being addressed by IT, consider bringing in a professional strategist. There are fractional CIO groups that are now able to share out the cost of a strategist, so that companies with more limited resources can take advantage of experienced pros. The difference between an IT person who fixes what's broken and an IT person who improves upon what's already working can be the difference between great service and award-winning excellence.

Disclosure: The author is an IT professional with twenty years of experience.

Accounting

The process improvement cycle may not have impacted your accounting team directly, but it can serve as a great guiding document for the team once it is complete. After all, it outlines the steps that must be taken in order for the company to succeed. Some of those steps have costs associated to them. Accounting can evaluate the costs and realized profit of each step, providing a real understanding of savings when the process improvement cycle reconvenes to revise and improve the documents.

The success of the company as reflected by the bottom line is directly evaluated by the Accounting team on a regular basis. No one is in a position to measure the success of the process improvement cycle like Accounting. While the team is often overlooked as insulated and performing only limited back office functions, in addition to seeming overworked and outside of the process, they are in fact the underpinning that can provide the most useful metrics and the best view into the productivity of the workforce.

In fact, the process improvement documents may be more guiding to Accounting than they are to anyone else. They can serve as an excellent roadmap for budgeting, and for planning headcount and other adjustments which impact reforecasts and variances throughout the year. The more insight Accounting has into the processes which run the company, the more the professionals can apply their learning and understanding to projecting the company's financial future.

If managers are in need of information about where the company is going, Accountants need to know how the company plans to get there. Process improvement documentation can be the way that the organization delivers that information.

Sales and Client Services

The most common work flowing starting place for a service organization is not in sales. This is probably because the sales team is seen in many companies as a mythical and heroic hunter, delivering the kill that supports the rest of the organization. Some companies even treat their sales organizations overtly as though their success comes straight from personality.

Of course, in many cases, the personality, tenacity and relationship skills of a sales person are what make the difference between moderate success and glowing productivity. Those star players should be more interested in the process output documents than almost anyone else in the firm.

The star salespeople with the amazing charisma will understand, without question, that their reputation is critical to their success. They can do the most amazing job aligning a customer with the right solution. They can even close the deal with both sides profiting from the venture. But salespeople, especially the great ones, typically do not implement solutions or act as customer service once the sale is closed.

The way that the company treats customers is a direct reflection upon the salesperson who values the relationship sales cycle. If they are to achieve repeat business, they have to without question ensure their customer is taken care of. Helping sales people understand the process improvement cycle that has been completed and what it means for customer interaction can be extremely beneficial and return information that otherwise might be overlooked.

From the other perspective, there is nearly nothing in the workplace that is more frustrating than having a salesperson promise something to a client which cannot be delivered by the service team. One of the keys to ensuring the coherent and peaceful coexistence of the sales and service sides of the business is strong understanding of what each side does. One way in which sales can stay informed about what service can actually do for clients is through the process documents.

TROUBLESHOOTING

Change Aversion

Having gone through a personal discovery process, a reinvigoration or establishment of a new corporate group dynamic, and the exhausting work of designing and documenting the company's workflows, you may be hoping to sit still for a few minutes.

Your organization needs your attention more than ever. In addition to helping with the adoption of the company's workflows, your attention is needed to keep the process improvement team together. After all, process design is not meant to simply memorialize a fixed point in time balance sheet reflection of where your company is at a given moment. You've created a starting point for your organization's growth.

Keeping the company on track is a manager's daily task. Energizing the workforce and instituting a culture of flexible creativity, respect and communication is enough for a full time job. The President or CEO needs to model the best behavior, ensuring that it flows gracefully down into the reaches of the organization.

Companies embrace new cultures differently and with varying success. Sometimes, after a process improvement cycle, there are changes that appear to happen as a result. Some executives, leaders or even employees are not able to slip into the new flow of things comfortably.

If your well-designed communication strategies have not quite taken yet, those who are having difficulty settling in might not feel comfortable bringing up their issues. This is not too difficult to handle by directly and compassionately bringing up topics that might help people feel more settled. Where it gets complicated is when the people having trouble adjusting have no idea they are struggling. Particularly when there are managers who are rudderless, employees can feel that they are being poorly treated. As always, insecurities in management work their way down to the staff. This kind of a situation can create a lot of tension, impede the adoption of the processes that have been designed, and cause problems that can impact production.

Human Resources should be prepared to step in and counsel employees who are not comfortable. HR should also have a route to senior leadership when there is the need to adjust the approach of a manager who may be causing discomfort on his staff.

Process Inconsistency

Occasionally, during the process improvement process, things will seem very clear. The steps taken to get from A to B will be validated by multiple people who should be in the know. And yet, when the process is released, it has zero resemblance to the way things are done. Worse, it doesn't really reflect how things should be done.

It's a good thing that process improvement is a constant flow of revision from learning. Reconvene. Update the process. Rerelease.

Lack of Compliance

There are two cases where you may perceive a lack of compliance. In one case, the employee truly does not understand what is expected. In that situation, the lack of compliance is actually an educational issue, and training should ensue. A review of the process can also be undertaken to determine where it could be more clear.

In the other case of what looks like non-compliance, an employee simply does not find that the process pertains to her. She may decide that she has a better way. In this case, the process review team owes it to the employee and the company to determine if her way is actually better. Where the documented process trumps the employee's ad hoc process, the employee must adapt and adopt the process.

Exception Sprawl

You've rolled out your processes. The adoption has gone well. Change management has happened as needed. You look up a year later and discover that there are more than a handful of exceptions to the written processes. In fact, almost every client represents an exception somewhere in the chain.

This could simply be indicative that something was wrong in the process to begin with. There are decision points missing that would otherwise show the options clients are being offered.

If the exceptions put the company at risk, however, there is the chance that the exception is trumped by the rule. The process as written must be followed, in these cases, or Human Resources must get involved to discipline the employees causing and authorizing the exceptions.

Over-Revision

After the emphasis this book has placed on the need to be consistently updating the processes that have been designed, it may be surprising for you to note that there can be over-revision to the process.

If your process improvement team is meeting more than once a month after the initial release of the process, you are probably meeting too often. The team meetings should wind down to roughly once a quarter by one year after release. This may be overkill for some companies that are not rapidly changing or diversifying.

If your process improvement team happens to be meeting so often because they have to, there is either a flaw in the process, or possibly a flaw in work distribution. Either way, oversight into the metrics that process improvement has provided you should allow you to adjust accordingly.

RESOURCES

KATHLEEN HURLEY

APPENDIX 1: POTENTIAL SERVICE COMPANY PROCESSES

PROCESS IMPROVEMENT FOR SERVICE BUSINESSES

Answering the Phone
Distributing the Mail
Engaging a New Client
Contracting for a Project
Contracting for Ongoing Services
Periodic Client Meetings (service &/or sales)
Beginning a Project
Taking on a New Client
Releasing Client Information
Renewing Contracts
Performing (Daily, Weekly, Monthly) Services
Internal Reporting

KATHLEEN HURLEY

APPENDIX 2: POTENTIAL SERVICE COMPANY ROLES

Reception
Sales Person
Sales Director
Service Coordinator
Service Manager
Human Resources
Administration
Marketing
Information Technology
Accounting
Client Services
Client Services Director
Legal or Contracts

APPENDIX 3: A SAMPLE MEMO ABOUT
COMMUNICATION OF TEAM PROCESS

PROCESS IMPROVEMENT FOR SERVICE BUSINESSES

Our company is undertaking a process improvement cycle. This is a groundbreaking investment in time and energy, and we welcome you to the process improvement team.

Your participation is critical to the success of our overall endeavor, which is to say, the success of our company in the future. We understand that you have a great deal of work which you have to attend to every day, and we appreciate the dedication of extra time and effort to the organization.

We anticipate such positive outcomes from this process, impacting the way we each work and serve our customers, that we want to insure our internal staff are as excited and as positive as we are about the undertaking.

The process improvement cycle will be transparent and will require, ultimately, input from the entire staff in order to be successful. As we move through the process, as you know if you have participated in such an endeavor before, there will be stops and starts and drafts which make sense to the process participants but might not make sense out of context.

When discussing the process improvement cycle with your colleagues who are not on the team, which you are strongly encouraged to do, please be aware of what statements can be helpful and encouraging and which statements could be confusing and worrisome.

KATHLEEN HURLEY

APPENDIX 4: THE WORK OF SETTING UP
THE PROCESS IMPROVEMENT CYCLE

1. Begin self-improvement cycle to prepare for the approach

2. Identify the best location for the team meetings

3. Identify the team to develop the mission, vision and values

4. Fill critical team roles

5. Prepare the mission, vision and values statements

6. Identify the team to prepare the process documents

7. Prepare the initial schedule in the proper format

8. Secure a communications coach if needed

9. Whole Org: discuss security of confidential and privileged and private information

APPENDIX 5: AFTER THE WORKFLOW IS COMPLETED

1. Review for checks and balances that can or should be inserted

2. Review notes from the meetings and about the workflows to see if anything was unused.

3. Review the workflows for tie-in to mission, vision and values

4. Capture innovation ideas from the meetings which were not incorporated into this workflow, but should be considered for future. Appoint project teams to research these ideas.

5. Schedule the team's next meeting

6. Communicate to senior leadership what the workflow team has produced, and use multimode communication to do so. Achieve a state of stakeholder adoption and avocation.

7. Communicate to middle management what the workflow team has produced, and use multimode communication. Achieve a state of knowledge transfer which will be implemented and adopted.

8. Survey

9. Continue to innovate and update.

10. Meet regularly to revise and update.

KATHLEEN HURLEY

APPENDIX 6:
THE RIGHT PERSON FOR THE RIGHT ROLE

PROCESS IMPROVEMENT FOR SERVICE BUSINESSES

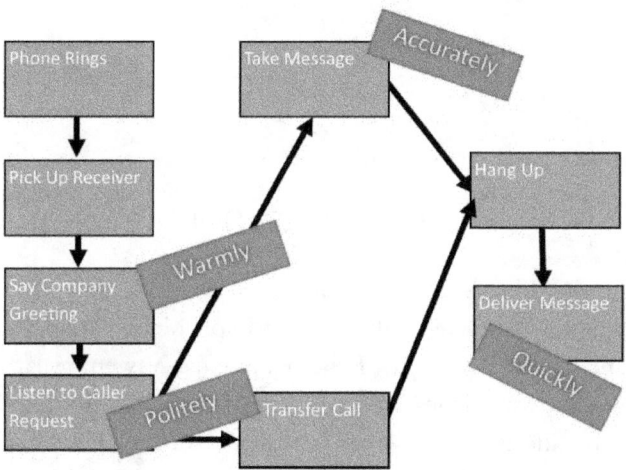

Filling a position based on a workflow is a manner of adding adjectives and adverbs to the designed workflow. This creates a picture of the skillset needed to properly fill a position.

Then structure your interview questions to seek out experiential information about the person's behavior. Are they prone to act in the way your adverbs and adjectives require?

KATHLEEN HURLEY

ABOUT THE AUTHOR

Kathleen Hurley studied English at Randolph-Macon Woman's College and The University of Reading. She has a twenty year background in strategic leadership in Information Technology and business operations, and received her MBA from the University of Wales. She's a fan of flow charts and grew up on TQM, has implemented many processes and is always thankful for the opportunity to dig into great systems and make them better.

In her spare time, Ms. Hurley loves traveling, particularly when she is able to see new places and meet new people. She reads obsessively, walks aimlessly and drinks coffee with abandon.

www.ingramcontent.com/pod-product-compliance
Lightning Source LLC
Chambersburg PA
CBHW060401190526
45169CB00002B/706